Nile

poems and photographs by

John Delaney

Finishing Line Press
Georgetown, Kentucky

Contents

Dedicated to Workers,
Ancient and Modern

*…and multiply my signs and my wonders
in the land of Egypt*

—Exodus vii.3

The Pyramids

In the sandy haze, the pyramids rise
like apparitions. There is nothing else
visible in this land of sand and rock
and rubble. They have spent a long time

acclimating to the harsh conditions.
It's hot and dry and gets unbearable,
but still they patiently impose their presence,
having prolonged the inevitable.

They challenge us to think big, to work hard
together, to take the long view.
They assume a kind of cheerleading role.
'You can do better. Make time count. Be true.'

When you stand close to the stone blocks
and touch their weathered skin, straining to see
the top, you wish your life could be
part of something as extraordinary.

*The oldest of the Seven Wonders of the Ancient World, the Great Pyramid
of Giza was built in the 26th century B.C., primarily of limestone. Granite
blocks in the King's Chamber weigh up to 80 tons. The structure is
approximately 2.5 football fields square, oriented to the four points of the
compass, almost 500 feet high, and consists of more than 2 million large
stone blocks.*

Hieroglyphics

A is a kind of vulture. B, the lower leg.
C is a cup with a handle. D, a glove or hand.
E, a flowering reed. F, a horned viper.
G is a jar stand. H is a courtyard.
I, the reed leaf again. J, a cobra.
K is the cup with the handle. L, a lion.
M is an owl. N is rippling water.
O, a rope with a noose. P, a mat or stool.
Q is a hillside. R is an open mouth.
S is a door bolt or a folded cloth.
T is a bread bun. U is a quail chick.
With V, the horned viper returns.
And so does the quail chick with W.
X needs the cup and the folded cloth.
Y, two of the reeds. And Z repeats
the door bolt (that looks like a belt buckle).

Well, those are sources of the letters' sounds.
But their pictures are worth a thousand words.

Hieroglyphics constituted the formal writing system of Ancient Egypt and were used to write the Egyptian language. About 1,000 distinct characters were used. Knowledge of the system was lost until it was deciphered in the 1820s with the help of the Rosetta Stone.

Tutankhamun

There's not a lot to say, strange as it seems.
I was a boy, expected to be king.
Yet I never got that far in my dreams.

They tell me my tomb was filled with treasure—
elaborate masks, furniture and toys,
some eighty pairs of golden sandals!

But I was mummified the same way:
a hook drew my brain out through my nostrils.
It was deemed useless in the Afterlife.

Other organs were removed and preserved in jars.
But not my heart, the seat of my soul.
It still had to pass the white feather test.

If your heart weighed less than the feather of truth,
you were judged a good man, welcomed to paradise.
I got an exemption, given my youth.

Tutankhamun, the Boy King popularly called "King Tut," ruled Egypt from 1332 to 1323 B.C., from the age of nine to nineteen. During his reign the traditional religion of Egypt was restored and the capital moved to Thebes. The cause of his death is still debated.

The Camel Market at Daraw

He clutches the baby camel
as if he'll never let him go.
But of course he will. One day. Here.
The camel's a commodity.

The older ones bunch in small groups
with hobbled forelegs. Men come by
and whack them on their haunches,
trying to gauge their meat with sticks.

The heat's becoming uncomfortable,
but the camels would never know it.
Most of the men talk at tables
in the shaded open-air huts.

The boy leaning on the palm tree
is this owner's teenage son,
listening to learn what it takes
to be the best camel trader.

The best advice is to love them,
holding them close for as long as you can—
the calf as well as the camel,
the boy who carries the man.

Daraw is one of the two large camel markets in Egypt. Most of the camels
come from Sudan and are sold for meat.

Abu Simbel

Holy Ramses! Twice built. Reassembled
precisely, piece by piece, on higher ground.

I wander around it like I once did
as a kid in Colonial Williamsburg,
where houses and workshops resurrect
a sense of place as it might have been;
re-enactors costumed in period dress
reinvent a past to make you believe.

Does it matter that the temple's been moved
from where it once held sway, formidable,
rock-cut? Can the statues project their power
with the same monumental face and force?

Who could really tell what is different?
The past is past but is always present.

*Constructed in the 13th century B.C. under the reign of Pharaoh Ramses
II, the temple was relocated to higher ground in the 1960s in a UNESCO
project to save it from the rising waters of Lake Nasser.*

The Box Maker of Fares

These hardy boxes of dried palm tree fronds
are mainly used to carry mangos
from harvest to market, their craftsman says.
His feet keep a stave moving as he talks,
seeming to punch holes without looking.
He's sixty-one and has been making these
for fifty years. About 4,000 a year,
as well as furniture and tourist trinkets.
So effortless and comfortable,
he works as if there's no such thing as work—
just satisfaction in doing something well.
It brings an income, has longevity:
everything that work can be if it has love,
and he labors with it as we listen.

Apparently, this man is well known in Egypt, for his mango boxes are seen up and down the Nile.

Dahabeya

The wind fights back against the current,
so these vessels have to tack or be pulled
by a tugboat to make headway downriver.
To us passengers, it doesn't matter—
a sense of drifting is what we're after.

The banks go by in a lazy rhythm
of buffet meals and shaded lounge chair chats,
as we cruise between ancient temple sites.
We try to imagine what's coming next
during our senior air-conditioned naps.

But most of all we drift in time and space.
Treated like pharaohs in their solar barques,
we're riding the Nile highway to heaven.
The bird on its thatch of sticks and grass,
just floating by, could say the same, even.

The Dahabeya is a type of luxury pleasure boat, reminiscent of royal travel, that commonly cruises between Aswan and Luxor on the Nile.

The Great Sphinx

The real riddle is what it sees
and has seen, even as time has fractured
its face. What is the view that so
captivates and motivates the viewer?

We who trespass in its vision
are blurred and out of focus,
too close and on the move. Nothing
distracts this hunter from its prey.

Nothing dissuades the eyes to blink,
the neck to turn, else something will be lost.
Its lips are sealed. Yet what magnetic field
locks a moment's gaze in an ageless stare?

*A mythical creature with the body of a lion and head of a human, the
Sphinx is one of the most recognizable statues in the world. It stands on
the west bank of the Nile, near the Giza pyramids.*

Heat

Such heat dresses you with its raiment
that keeps adjusting to your shape
until it starts to be a burden
that you carry, all enveloping,
like a burkha with a slit for your eyes
that you peer through for another step
in the haze that's becoming a curtain
heavy to part, where once inside,
you begin the process of undressing,
layer by layer, with chilling effect.

Egypt has a hot desert climate and is exceedingly dry over most of the country, except along the Mediterranean.

The Galabeya Tailor of Esna

Galabeya, sounds like it spells—
the standard dress of a working
Egyptian man, whether in the fields
or the shops. Long and loose-fitting.
The old tailor wears one himself.

Two blocks from the Temple of Knum,
god of the source of the Nile,
he works at his Singer machine,
shoeless and nimble-fingered,
sewing the seams of the garment.

Not fashion, not a uniform.
An everyday necessity
no one has to think what to wear.
Go in the shop and pick your cloth.
Get measured for a custom fit.

Wrap a turban round your head
to highlight the nobility,
so, when it's ready, you can walk out
among your peers dressed like a god
who has garbed responsibilities on Earth.

In the hot summer a white Galabeya is common; winter colors include grey, tan, olive, and shades of blue.

Karnak

Temple upon temple upon temple,
gated fortresses of the spirit,
some yet to be discovered. A mental

walk among the crowds and ruins,
savoring the scent of ancient stone.
I looked up at the towering columns

and imagined one slightly off-balance,
slowly tipping, setting off a cascading
fall of dominoes; by a second glance,

though, they still stood solidly attentive
to their hieroglyphic narratives
in which, for centuries, they have lived,

both lifting and bearing the messages.
I was led to believe that something
as unwavering always blesses us,

cupping brilliant sunlight in my hands.

*An overwhelming complex of temples, Karnak dates from the 19th to the
3rd centuries B.C. Included are numerous statues, an obelisk, and a hall of
over 130 columns. Excavation continues.*

Valley of the Kings

A cemetery unlike any other.
Tourists wait in line to descend the stairs
that lead to lavish vaults where ancient kings
received their send-offs to the Afterlife.
Some are multi-chambered; all tell stories.
Emptied now of treasures and their mummies,
the tombs are decorated anterooms.

We, too, hope that certain ceremonies
and memorials preserve the memories
of what each person requires ahead.
We bury them in coffins underground;
we burn their bodies on funeral pyres;
we spread their ashes all around—
seeking how best to bid goodbye to the dead.

For over 500 years, on the west bank of the Nile, opposite Thebes (now Luxor), where the sun goes to die, Egyptians buried their kings in these elaborate sealed tombs.

The Nile

Time, the river, winds the length of Egypt.
So much is asked of it, so much given.

Hemmed in by the desert's desolation,
it fertilized pharaonic fantasy.

Its bulrushes hid the baby Moses,
prophet of the Bible's Exodus.

Sandwiched by sand and toasted by heat,
it's offered a verdant, varied relief.

Cattle graze along its banks; men harvest
irrigated crops of wheat and sugarcane.

What once transported quarried limestone blocks
now plies itineraries for tourist stops.

Aswan, Edfu, Esna, Luxor, Cairo:
it's quenched the thirst of their pasts and present.

There would be no Egypt without the Nile.
There would be no life without its water.
And there would be no time—without its when, its while.

The White Nile from Lake Victoria in Kenya and the Blue Nile from Lake Tana in Ethiopia join at Khartoum, Sudan. From there the Nile flows north through Sudan and Egypt to the Mediterranean.

Field workers in their galabeyas harvesting wheat
in the coolness of early morning

John at Tutankhamun's Tomb
[photograph by Susan Delaney]

John Delaney retired after 35 years in the Dept. of Rare Books and Special Collections of Princeton University Library, where he was head of manuscripts processing and then, for the last 15 years, curator of historic maps. He's written a number of works on cartography, including *Strait Through: Magellan to Cook and the Pacific*; *First X, Then Y, Now Z: An Introduction to Landmark Thematic Maps*; and *Nova Caesarea: A Cartographic Record of the Garden State, 1666-1888*. These have extensive website versions.

He's been writing poems for most of his life, and, in the 1970s, attended the Writing Program of Syracuse University, where his mentors were poets W. D. Snodgrass and Philip Booth. In subtle ways, they have bookended his approach to poems. In 2017, John published *Waypoints*, a collection of place poems. *Twenty Questions*, a chapbook, appeared in 2019, and *Delicate Arch: Poems and Photographs of National Parks and Monuments* was published in 2022. A trip to the Galápagos archipelago with his son Andrew in 2021 resulted in the chapbook *Galápagos* (2023), consisting of his son's color photographs and John's poetic responses. John has traveled widely, preferring remote, natural settings, and makes his home in Port Townsend, WA.

A Note About This Book

This book is the result of a 15-day tour of Egypt that I took with my sister Susan and a small group of fellow travelers in April 2022. It was hot and dry and stunning. Like most foreign travelers there, we expected to be awed at the way such ancient history survives and informs the fabric of modern Egyptian life. And we were.